EQUINOX

Seasonally Inspired Petit Gateaux

CHEF KRISTIN BRANGWYNNE

Photography by Justin Kaicles

To order additional copies of this book, contact:
Xlibris
844-714-8691
www.Xlibris.com
Orders@Xlibris.com

ISBN: Softcover   978-1-6698-0823-7
         Hardcover   978-1-6698-0824-4
         EBook   978-1-6698-0822-0

Library of Congress Control Number: 2022901457

Print information available on the last page.

Rev. date: 01/26/2022

If you are looking for a dessert book with light flavorful creations to end a delightful meal with, then you have found what you are looking for. Equinox was created by Kristin Brangwynne to fascinate and fulfill even the most demanding foodies through out the four seasons. Kristin was a student of mine at The Culinary Institute of America in Hyde Park, NY. Since graduating with a Bachelors degree in food service management, Kristin has worked in high-end hotels and resorts honing her skills and perfecting formulas to create this tantalizing book.

This book on seasonal entremets should be a great addition to anyone's book collection. From a novice home baker to a seasoned pastry chef, all can benefit from the various formulas and techniques used throughout this book. Once you have tried some of these formulas, you too will start to understand how complex flavor combinations and textures comingle to create delectable delights.

Thank you for including me in this project, I can't wait to see what you create next!

Joseph Utera CMB, CEPC, M.Ed.

Professor

The Culinary Institute of America

Hyde Park NY

I have had the pleasure of working with Kristin Brangwynne twice now and with 25 years of experience I have worked with my share of pastry chefs. We first met during my tenure at the Gaylord Opryland Resort and Convention Center. Her calm demeanor and presence in the kitchen allowed her to navigate the high-volume stresses of the megalithic resort with relative ease. It was here that she truly began developing her creative style and technical skills.

In the fall of 2019, I was given the opportunity to develop a team and help open the privately owned, luxury hotel, The Grand Hyatt Nashville. The level of quality at this hotel demanded talent that I had only previously seen in Kristin. I brought her downtown and pleaded with her to help me open the hotel. She eagerly joined the team and immediately began to set the bar on a pastry program that I will remember for years to come. Refining her skills there has led Kristin to embark on a new challenge of putting together this book. A reflection of her early years to the current period of her truly beginning to define herself, this book will be a welcome addition to your collection. It is a privilege to see her hard work put together in a collection like this. Kristin, you should be proud of this and I am truly honored to be a part of it.

Brian Owenby

Seeing Kristin hone her talents over the years has been an absolute treat – pun intended. Her creations continue to astound me with flavor combinations and visual presentations creating works of art that taste even better than they look. I know this book will be the first in a long line and I can't wait to see what comes out next. I am so proud of you and I love you Kristin.

Amanda Brangwynne

I have been lucky enough to watch Kristin evolve from a budding young baker to an inspired and innovative professional pastry chef. As Kristin's younger sister, I was her built in "taste-tester" for her numerous creations growing up. From her signature snicker doodle cookies to intricate pastries, Kristin has a special ability to place anyone who was lucky enough to try her creation in absolute awe. There is genuinely nothing in this world that I love more than eating the pastries Kristin creates. Not only because of their phenomenal taste, but also because of the passion, effort and talent that I know Kristin puts into creating such beautiful designs and complex flavor patterns. I will forever be Kristin's biggest supporter and I am beyond excited to be a part of this project. I could not be more proud of everything Kristin has accomplished and this recipe book is only a tiny fraction of her amazing past and future achievements. I love you so much, Kristin!

Erica Brangwynne

This book is a physical representation of the love and passion I have for pastry. Growing up I had always wanted to be an artist. My grandfather was an artist and I found inspiration for my sketches from his artwork. However, I owe my discovery in the world of pastry to my mom. After helping her out in the kitchen making desserts for special occasions and family events I realized exactly what I wanted to do. I was about 14 years old. Combining art and pastry I was able to fine-tune my interests into a career.

Once my career path was set I was determined to put in the work and learn as much as I could. That is the beautiful thing about the food industry is that there are always new paths to explore and the creative opportunities are endless. With the exceptional classes and chef instructors at the Culinary Institute of America and all of my wonderful chefs and mentors at Gaylord Opryland Resort, Grand Hyatt Nashville and M Street Entertainment I was able to push myself to start taking on my own visions of pastries and making them a reality. Being able to excite and intrigue people with dessert is what drives my work. The ability to share my work with friends and family is a truly special thing. That is what I am hoping to give with this book. Allowing everyone to challenge him or herself and create new memories with pastry as I have. Yes, I am professionally trained, however every single pastry in this book I created in a home kitchen. With the right attitude, patience and willingness to try and fail then try again, you will be surprised at how much you are able to accomplish. Trust yourself and I know with full confidence that you too are a pastry chef.

Ever since I was little I wanted to write a book. I would write the goofiest little picture books all of which my amazing parents have saved. This completed, published book is completely dedicated to you, Jim and Fadia. The most supportive, loving, all around best parents I could ever have. I love you both so much. This one's for you.

SPRING

Spring brings freshness. The winter chill has thawed giving us a variety of flavor combinations to exhibit this season. I chose to use a lot of herbs in the spring pastries paired with the simple, fresh tastes and textures of specific fruits. This chapter features light colors, fresh flavors and simplistic ingredient pairings to really capture the simple elegance that this season provides.

Pineapple Rosemary

Rosemary Sablé

AP flour	100 g
Salt	1 g
Butter	60 g
Powdered sugar	38 g
Ground almonds	13 g
Eggs	22 g
Rosemary sprig	1 ea

Bloom gelatin in ice water. Combine pineapple juice and sugar in a pot, bring to a boil. Pour into yolks, whisking constantly, and return to the heat. Cook until thickened. Add in gelatin. Add in butter. Cool, stir in cubed pineapple.

Pineapple Curd

Pineapple juice	180 g
Sugar	180 g
Egg yolks	8 ea
Butter	120 g
Gelatin	3 ea
Cubed pineapple	½ C

Bloom gelatin in ice water. Combine milk, ½ sugar and vanilla in a pot, bring to a boil. Temper into egg yolks, whisking to combine. Return to the heat, stir and cook until mixture reaches 189F. Add in bloomed gelatin, set aside to cool. Whip cream, fold with milk mixture.

Vanilla Bavarois

Egg yolks	6 ea
Vanilla bean	1 ea
Sugar	100 g
Milk	480 g
Gelatin	6 ea
Cream	500 g

Combine egg whites and cream of tartar in a bowl with a whip. Slowly add in sugar until medium peaks are achieved. Fold in almond flour and powdered sugar. Spread on a baking sheet with parchment paper. Bake at 350F for 12-15min.

Almond Dacquoise

Egg whites	375 g
Cream of tartar	3 g
Sugar	90 g
Almond flour	300 g
Powdered sugar	300 g

Combine flour, almonds, salt, butter and rosemary in a bowl. Mix until combined.
Add in powdered sugar and eggs. Mix until dough forms.
Wrap and chill for 2 hours.
Bake at 380F for 10-15min or until the edges are golden.

Chantilly

Cream	200 g
Powdered sugar	75 g
Vanilla bean	1 ea

Combine all ingredients in a bowl. Whip until stiff peaks are formed.

Candied Rosemary

Rosemary sprigs	12 ea
Sugar	1 C

Dip rosemary sprigs in water and toss in sugar. Lay out on parchment to dry out, about 1 hour.

Yellow Glaze

White chocolate	350 g
Water	150 g
Sugar	200 g
Condensed milk	300 g
Gelatin	18 g
Vanilla	1 tbsp
Yellow color	as needed

Bloom gelatin in ice water.
Combine water, sugar, vanilla and condensed milk in a pot. Bring to a boil. Add in bloomed gelatin, pour over white chocolate. Add in food color. Combine until homogenous.

Assembly Instructions:
1. Make and bake almond dacquoise, freeze.
2. Make pineapple curd, spread on a plastic wrap lined sheet tray, freeze.
3. Punch out cake and curd with desired cutter once they are frozen.
4. Make vanilla bavarois, pipe into desired mold. Press in pineapple curd and dacquoise, freeze until solid.
5. Bake rosemary sablé, set aside.
6. Unmold vanilla bavarois, glaze with yellow glaze, transfer onto rosemary sablé base.
7. Pipe on chantilly
8. Place sugared rosemary sprig and cubed pineapple.

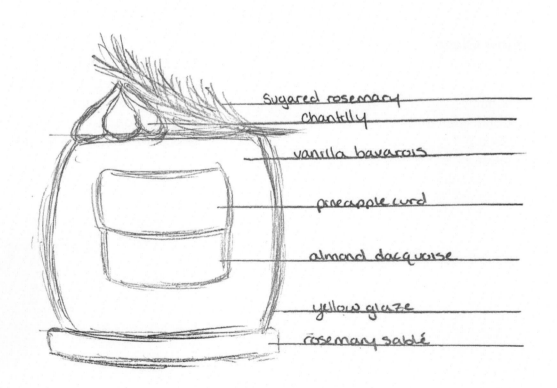

sugared rosemary
chantilly
vanilla bavarois
pineapple curd
almond dacquoise
yellow glaze
rosemary sablé

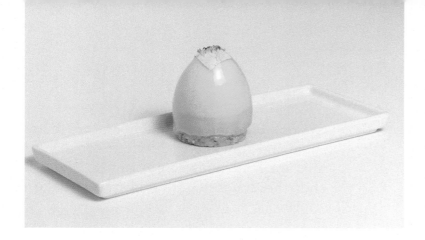

Olive Oil and Orange

Olive Oil Mousse

White chocolate	284 g
Eggs, separated	8 ea
Sugar	170 g
Olive oil	113 g
Orange zest	1 tbsp
Salt	¼ tsp
Gelatin	6 ea

Bloom gelatin in ice water. Melt chocolate, set aside. Whip egg yolks and 113g of sugar until pale yellow and fluffy. Add in olive oil, salt and zest. Melt and stir in gelatin. Fold in white chocolate. Whip egg whites while gradually adding in remaining sugar until medium peaks form. Fold meringue with olive oil mixture.

Pistachio Joconde

Almond flour	105 g
Raw pistachios	105 g
Powdered sugar	150 g
AP flour	50 g
Eggs	250 g
Egg whites	185 g
Sugar	75 g
Butter, melted	25 g

Place pistachios, powdered sugar and almond flour in a food processor, pulse until it forms a fine powder. Mix with AP flour and whole eggs. Whip until pale and aerated. Whip up egg whites while streaming in sugar until medium peaks form. Fold meringue into almond mixture. Fold in melted butter, spread onto a parchment lined tray. Bake at 375F for about 12 minutes.

Orange Curd

Orange juice	180 g
Sugar	180 g
Egg yolks	8 ea
Butter	120 g
Gelatin	5 ea

Bloom gelatin in ice water. Place sugar and orange juice in a pot. Bring to a boil. Whisk in egg yolks. Return to heat, whisk constantly until thickened. Add in bloomed gelatin. Add in cubed butter.

Pistachio Crumble

AP flour	280 g
Butter	200 g
Ground pistachios	250 g
Orange zest	1 tbsp
Sugar	240 g

Cream together room temperature butter, sugar and orange zest. Sift flour, add to butter mixture. Fold in pistachio crumbs. Wrap and chill the dough. Grate and freeze. Bake at 300F.

Orange Glaze

White chocolate	350 g
Water	150 g
Sugar	200 g
Condensed milk	300 g
Gelatin	18 g
Vanilla	1 tbsp
Orange food color	as needed

Bloom gelatin in ice water. Combine water, sugar, vanilla and condensed milk in a pot. Bring to a boil. Add in bloomed gelatin, pour over white chocolate. Add in orange color, mix until homogeneous.

Assembly Instructions:

1. Make and bake pistachio joconde. Let cool.
2. Make olive oil mousse, fill the desired mold halfway. Freeze.
3. Punch out a sized round of pistachio joconde to fit inside the mold. Press joconde on top of olive oil mousse, return to the freezer.
4. Make orange curd; pour over pistachio joconde in mold to fill the remainder of the space. Freeze until solid.
5. Take the grated, frozen pistachio crumble, press into rounds to make the base of the petit gateaux. Bake at 300F for about 10-12 minutes.
6. Unmold petit gateaux onto a glazing rack. Glaze with the light orange glaze.
7. Place on the cooled pistachio crumble base.
8. Garnish with gold leaf.

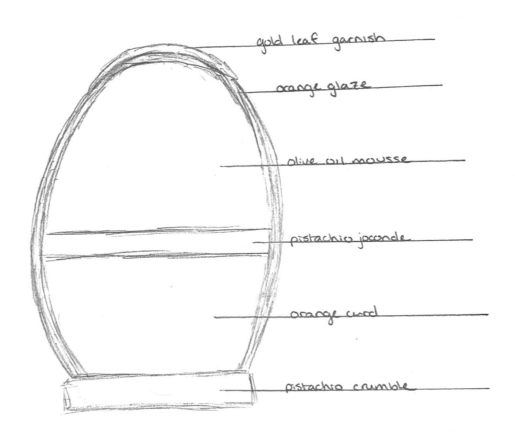

Mango Basil

Mango Mousse

Gelatin sheets	4 ea	
Eggs	3 ea	
Sugar (A)	125 g	
Mango puree	125 g	
Lemon juice	1 tsp	
Egg Whites	130 g	
Sugar (B)	100 g	

Bloom gelatin in ice water. Combine sugar (A), mango puree and lemon juice in a pot. Bring to a boil. Pour mango mix into eggs while whisking constantly. Return mixture to the heat. Cook, whisking continuously until thickened. Add in bloomed gelatin, set aside to cool.

Place egg whites on a mixer with a whip attachment. Whip while gradually adding in sugar (B) until medium peaks form. Fold mango mixture with meringue.

Basil Cremeux

Basil Leaves	6 ea	
Cream	250 g	
Egg yolks	80 g	
Sugar	60 g	
Gelatin	4 ea	
Vanilla	10 g	

Bloom gelatin in ice water. Steep basil leaves in cream on low heat for about 30min. Strain out basil leaves. Combine cream, sugar and vanilla in a pot. Bring to a boil. Temper the cream mixture into the egg yolks, whisking constantly. Return the mix to the heat. Cook until it reaches 189F while stirring. Add in bloomed gelatin.

Mango Compote

Mango chunks	1 ea	
Sugar	55 g	
Lemon juice	2 tbsp	
Vanilla Bean	1 ea	

Combine all ingredients in a pot. Cook for about 10min, stir often.

Lemon Basil Chiboust

Cream	220 g
Basil leaves	3 ea
Lemon zest	1 ea
Vanilla bean	1 ea
Egg yolks	80 g
Sugar (A)	30 g
Gelatin	16 g
Egg whites	140 g
Sugar (B)	100 g

Bloom gelatin in ice water. Steep basil and lemon zest in cream on low heat. Strain out. Combine cream, sugar (A) and vanilla in a pot, bring to a boil. Pour into egg yolks, whisking constantly. Return to heat, cook mixture until thickened. Add in bloomed gelatin, set aside to cool. Whip egg whites on mixer while gradually adding in sugar (B) until stiff peaks form. Fold with basil mixture.

Graham Sablé

Butter	114 g
Salt	1 g
Sugar	99 g
Vanilla	28 g
Graham cracker	113 g
AP flour	212 g
Cinnamon	3 g
Baking powder	4 g
Egg yolks	30 g

Cream butter and sugar. Add in egg yolks, vanilla and salt. Mix until combined. Sift and add in dry ingredients. Add in graham cracker crumbs. Mix until a dough forms. Wrap and chill dough for 1 hour before use. Roll to ⅛" and cut the desired shape. Bake at 325F for about 8-10 minutes.

Glaze

White chocolate	350 g
Water	150 g
Sugar	200 g
Condensed milk	300 g
Gelatin	18 g
Vanilla	1 tbsp
Food color	as needed

Bloom gelatin in ice water. Combine water, sugar and condensed milk in a pot. Bring to a boil. Add in bloomed gelatin. Pour over white chocolate. Add in food color, mix until homogeneous.

Assembly Instructions:
1. Make basil cremeux; pour into a small insert mold. Freeze until solid.
2. Make mango compote; pour into a medium insert mold. Freeze until solid.
3. Unmold inserts.
4. Make mango mousse, pour into medium mold, press in basil cremeux insert. Freeze until solid.
5. Make lemon basil chiboust, pour into a large mold, press in mango compote insert. Freeze until solid.
6. Make glaze, glaze half green and half orange.
7. Unmold lemon basil chiboust, glaze with green glaze, and set on graham sablé base.
8. Unmold mango mousse, glaze with orange glaze. Set on top of the glazed lemon basil chiboust.
9. Garnish with tempered white chocolate flowers if desired.

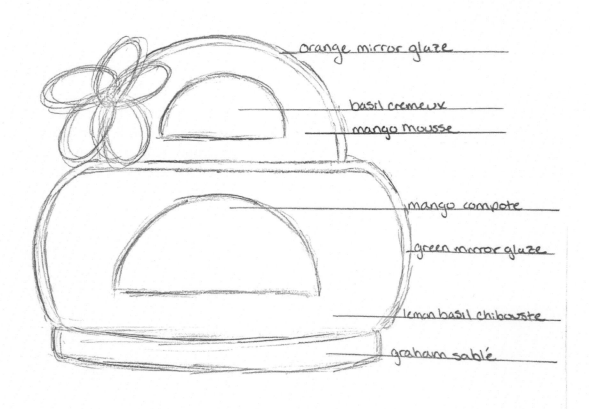

orange mirror glaze

basil cremeux

mango mousse

mango compote

green mirror glaze

lemon basil chibouste

graham sablé

Hazelnut Coffee

Hazelnut Mousse

Hazelnuts	1½ C	
Powdered Sugar	173 g	
Egg white	1 ea	
Milk	217 g	
Cream	168 g	
Sugar	50 g	
Vanilla bean	1 ea	
Egg yolks	4 ea	
Gelatin	3 ea	
Whipped cream	210 g	

Combine hazelnuts, powdered sugar and egg white in a food processor. Pulse until a paste forms, set aside. Bloom gelatin in ice water. Place milk, cream and vanilla bean in a pot. Bring to a boil. Temper mix into egg yolks. Return to heat and cook until the temperature reaches 189F, stirring occasionally. Add in bloomed gelatin. Pour over hazelnut paste, mix to combine. Fold with whipped cream.

Cherry Compote

Cherries	500 g
Sugar	200 g
Vanilla	20 g
Lemon juice	15 g
Cornstarch	5 g
Water	2 g

Combine cherries, sugar, vanilla and lemon juice in a pot. Cook until cherries get soft. Create a slurry with the cornstarch and water, stir into the cherry mixture. Cook until thickened.

Coffee Pastry Cream

Milk	159 g
Cream	97 g
Vanilla	1 tbsp
Instant coffee	50 g
Egg yolks	76 g
Sugar	31 g

Combine coffee powder, milk, cream and vanilla in a pot. Bring to a boil. Whisk into yolks and sugar, return the mixture to the heat. Whisk until thickened.

Red Glaze

White chocolate	350 g
Water	150 g
Sugar	200 g
Condensed Milk	300 g
Gelatin	18 g
Vanilla	1 tbsp
Red food color	as needed

Bloom gelatin in ice water.
Combine water, sugar, vanilla and condensed milk in a pot. Bring to a boil. Add in bloomed gelatin, pour over white chocolate. Add in red food color, mix until homogeneous.

Assembly Instructions:

1. Cook cherry compote, spread on a plast ic wrap lined tray. Freeze until solid.
2. Cook coffee pastry cream, pour over frozen cherry compote. Freeze until solid.
3. Cut out inserts from the cherry compote and coffee pastry cream with the chosen cutter.
4. Make hazelnut mousse, pour into desired mold, and press in cherry coffee insert. Freeze until solid.
5. Once frozen, unmold petit gateaux onto a glazing rack. Glaze with red glaze.
6. Press feuilletine around the base of the desert.
7. Garnish with hazelnut tuile, tempered white chocolate discs and halved cherries.

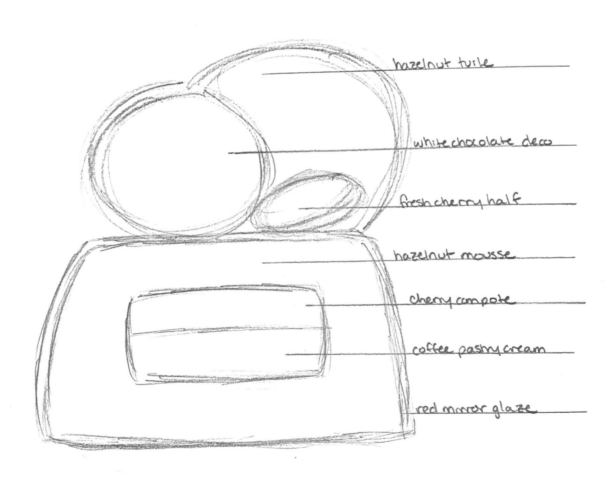

Guava Vanilla

Vanilla Chiboust

Milk	165 g
Cream	96 g
Vanilla bean	1 ea
Egg yolks	80 g
Sugar (A)	34 g
Gelatin	18 g
Egg whites	136 g
Sugar (B)	106 g

Bloom gelatin in ice water. Combine milk, cream and vanilla bean in a pot. Bring to a boil. Whisk into egg yolks and sugar (A), return mixture to heat. Cook until thickened, whisking constantly. Add in bloomed gelatin. Whip egg whites while gradually adding in sugar (B) until medium peaks form. Fold meringue with cream mixture.

Guava Curd

Butter	170 g
Guava puree	170 g
Sugar	360 g
Eggs	127 g
Gelatin	2 ea

Bloom gelatin in ice water. Combine guava puree and sugar in a pot. Bring to a boil. Whisk in eggs. Cook until thickened, whisking constantly. Remove from heat, add in bloomed gelatin. Add in butter, mix until smooth.

Guava Diplomat

Milk	80 g
Cream	48 g
Guava puree	70 g
Vanilla	1 tbsp
Egg yolks	40 g
Sugar	15 g
Whipped cream	200 g

Combine milk, cream, puree and vanilla in a pot. Bring to a boil. Whisk in egg yolks and sugar. Cook until thickened, whisking constantly. Fold in whipped cream.

Graham Sablé

Butter	114 g
Salt	1 g
Sugar	99 g
Vanilla	28 g
Graham cracker	113 g
AP flour	212 g
Cinnamon	3 g
Baking powder	4 g
Egg yolks	30 g

Cream butter and sugar. Add in egg yolks, vanilla and salt. Mix until combined. Sift together dry ingredients. Add into the butter mixture. Add in graham cracker crumbs. Mix until a dough forms. Wrap and chill for 1 hour. Roll to ⅛" and cut. Bake at 325F for about 6-8 min.

Vanilla Bean Glaze

White chocolate	350 g
Water	150 g
Sugar	200 g
Condensed milk	300 g
Gelatin	18 g
Vanilla bean	1 ea

Bloom gelatin in ice water. Combine water, sugar, vanilla bean and condensed milk in a pot. Bring to a boil. Add in bloomed gelatin, pour over white chocolate. Emulsify until smooth.

Guava Meringue

Egg whites	60 g
Sugar	150 g
Water	50 g
Guava Puree	50 g

Place egg whites on a mixer fitted with a whip attachment. Combine sugar and water in a pot. Cook to 240F. Stream hot sugar into whipping egg whites on high speed. Whip until stiff, shiny peaks form. Stir in guava puree.

Assembly Instructions:

1. Make guava curd, pipe into desired insert mold. Freeze until solid.
2. Unmold guava curd
3. Make vanilla chiboust, pipe into desired mold, press in guava curd. Freeze until solid.
4. Line tart shells with graham sablé. Bake at 325F for about 10-12 minutes.
5. Make guava diplomat cream, pipe into cooled tart shells.
6. Unmold chiboust onto a glazing rack, glaze with vanilla bean glaze. Press the feuilletine around the base.
7. Transfer petit gateaux onto a filled tart shell.
8. Pipe guava meringue rosette on top.
9. Top with edible gold leaf.

Coconut Strawberry

Coconut Chiboust

Coconut milk	160 g
Cream	94 g
Vanilla bean	1 ea
Egg yolks	76 g
Sugar (A)	33 g
Gelatin	16 g
Egg whites	135 g
Sugar (B)	104 g

Bloom gelatin in ice water. Combine milk, cream and vanilla bean in a pot, Bring to a boil. Temper into egg yolks and sugar (A) whisking vigorously. Return mixture to the heat. Cook until thickened, whisking constantly. Add in bloomed gelatin. Whip egg whites while gradually adding in sugar (B) until medium peaks form. Fold with coconut milk mixture.

Strawberry Curd

Strawberries	1 C
Lemon juice	1 tbsp
Egg yolks	3 ea
Sugar	100 g
Butter	57 g

Combine strawberries and lemon juice in a pot, cook down then blend to a puree. Return to pot with the sugar, bring to a boil. Add in egg yolks, cook until thickened while whisking constantly. Remove from heat and add in butter.

Coconut Tuile

Butter	28 g
Sugar	71 g
Corn syrup	18 g
Water	21 g
AP flour	38 g
Desiccated coconut	35 g

Preheat the oven to 400F. Paddle butter until very soft on a low setting so not to aerate it. Add in sugar, corn syrup and water, paddle until combined. Add in flour, mix to combine. Fold in coconut. Place mixture in a piping bag. Line a tray with silpat or parchment paper. Pipe the dough to about the size of a nickel allowing enough space between cookies. Bake for about 6-8 minutes or until the cookies are flat and caramelized.

Glaze

White chocolate	350 g
Water	150 g
Sugar	200 g
Condensed milk	300 g
Gelatin	18 g
Vanilla	1 tbsp
Pink food color	as needed

Bloom gelatin in ice water. Combine water, sugar, vanilla and condensed milk in a pot, bring to a boil. Add in bloomed gelatin. Pour mixture over white chocolate. Add in pink food color, mix until homogeneous.

Chantilly

Cream	200 g
Powdered sugar	75 g
Vanilla bean	1 ea

Combine all ingredients in a bowl. Whip until medium/stiff peaks form.

Assembly Instructions
1. Make strawberry curd. Pipe into desired insert mold. Freeze until solid.
2. Unmold curd
3. Make coconut chiboust, pipe into desired mold, and press in strawberry curd. Freeze until solid.
4. Unmold petit gateaux onto a glazing rack. Glaze with lig.ht pink glaze.
5. Press desiccated coconut around the base of the dessert.
6. Press desiccated coconut around the base of the dessert.
7. Place coconut tuile on top of the desert followed by a rosette of chantilly and a cross section of strawberry.

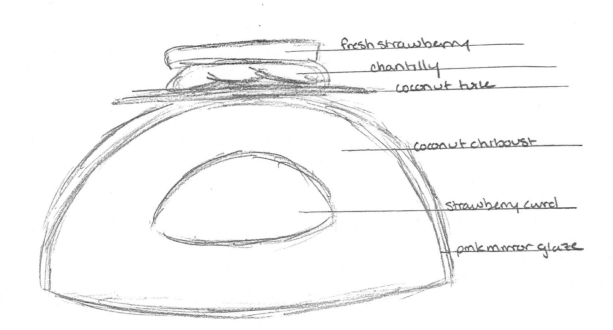

fresh strawberry
chantilly
coconut tuile
coconut chiboust
strawberry curd
pink mirror glaze

SUMMER

The hot months of summer create the desire for strong and vibrant desserts. The heat brings out more exotic and tropical flavors. I worked to incorporate some more traditional flavor combinations that come to mind when thinking of summer but also worked to include some unique and thought provoking looks and ingredients.

Strawberry Peach

Vanilla Cheesecake

Cream cheese	8 oz
Lemon zest	1 tsp
Vanilla bean	1 ea
Egg	1 ea
Sugar	50 g
Salt	¼ tsp
Cornstarch	1 tbsp

Preheat the oven to 325°F. In a bowl combine cream cheese, sugar, zest, salt and vanilla bean. Mix until smooth. Add in the egg and cornstarch. Pour into desired pan. Bake until firm.

Peach Jam

Peaches	3 ea
Water	60 g
Brown sugar	80 g
Vanilla	1 tbsp
Lemon juice	½ tbsp
Gelatin	2 ea

Bloom gelatin in ice water, set aside. Peel and dice peaches. Combine all ingredients in a pot. Cook until the peaches are tender. Add in bloomed gelatin. Emulsify until smooth.

Strawberry Mousse

Strawberries	½ C
Lemon juice	½ tbsp
Sugar	50 g
Egg yolks	2 ea
Gelatin	16 g
Whipped cream	225 g

Bloom gelatin in ice water, set aside. Dice strawberries and place in a pot. Cook until the berries are soft, blend into a puree. Add strawberry puree, lemon juice and sugar in a pot, bring to a boil. Temper into egg yolks, return to the heat. Whisk constantly until the mixture becomes thick. Add in bloomed gelatin, set aside to cool. Fold with whipped cream

Glaze

White chocolate	350 g
Water	150 g
Sugar	300 g
Gelatin	18 g
Condensed milk	300 g
Food color	as needed

Bloom gelatin in ice water, set aside. Combine water, sugar and condensed milk in a pot, bring to a boil. Add in bloomed gelatin. Pour mixture over white chocolate. Add in yellow food coloring. Emulsify until smooth.

Assembly Instructions
1. Make and bake vanilla cheesecake, freeze until solid.
2. Make peach jam, pour into desired mold. Freeze until solid.
3. Make strawberry mousse, pour into the mold.
4. Punch out peach jam insert, press into strawberry mousse. Freeze until solid.
5. Make white glaze and pink glaze.
6. Unmold vanilla cheesecake and glaze with the white glaze.
7. Unmold petit gateau and glaze with the pink glaze.
8. Stack cheesecake on top of the strawberry.
9. Garnish with dehydrated strawberry slice.

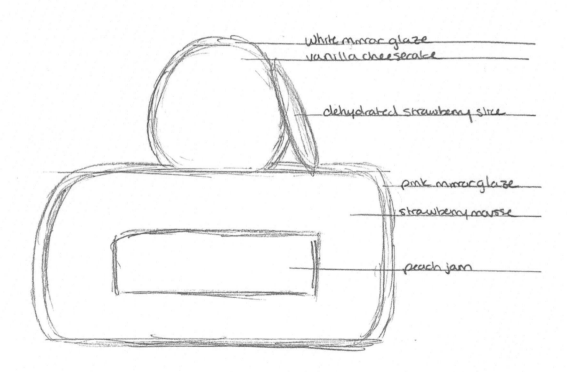

white mirror glaze
vanilla cheesecake

dehydrated strawberry slice

pink mirror glaze
strawberry mousse

peach jam

Pina Colada

Pineapple Mousse

Pineapple puree	250 g
Heavy cream	250 g
Egg yolks	80 g
Sugar	60 g
Gelatin	10 g
Whipped cream	500 g

Bloom gelatin in ice water, set aside. Boil cream. In a separate bowl whisk together egg yolks and sugar. Temper hot cream into yolk mixture, return to the heat. Cook to 189°F stirring constantly. Add in bloomed gelatin. Fold mix into pineapple puree, allow to cool. Whip and fold in whipped cream.

Coconut Pastry Cream

Coconut milk	456 g
Sugar	75 g
Salt	pinch
Cornstarch	19 g
Vanilla bean	1 ea
Egg yolk	3 ea
Whole egg	1 ea
Butter	60 g
Gelatin	4 ea

Bloom gelatin in ice water, set aside. Place coconut milk and vanilla bean in a pot, bring to a boil. In a separate bowl whisk together sugar, cornstarch, egg yolks and whole egg. Temper milk into egg mix, return to the heat. Cook, whisking constantly, until thickened. Add in bloomed gelatin. Whisk in butter.

Rum Syrup

Rum	120 g
Water	180 g
Brown sugar	110 g
Orange peel	1 ea
Orange juice	50 g
Cinnamon sticks	3 ea
All spice	½ tsp
Cloves	1 tsp

Combine all ingredients in a pot. Simmer for 30 minutes.

Baba

Yeast	1 tsp
Warm milk	3 tbsp
AP flour	300 g
Sugar	100 g
Baking powder	10 g
Egg yolks	3 ea
Egg whites	3 ea
Melted butter	50 g

Combine yeast and warm milk in a bowl, set aside. Cream sugar and egg yolks. Add milk mix, flour, butter and baking powder to the yolk mix. In a separate bowl, whip egg whites to medium peaks. Fold with egg yolk mixture. Spread onto a baking sheet. Bake at 350°F for 20-25 minutes. Inject rum syrup into baba cake to soak.

Glaze

White chocolate	350 g
Condensed milk	200 g
Sugar	300 g
Water	250 g
Gelatin	18 g
Vanilla	1 tbsp
Food color	as needed

Bloom gelatin in ice water. Combine water, sugar, vanilla and condensed milk in a pot, bring to a boil. Add in bloomed gelatin. Pour mixture over white chocolate. Add in pink food color, mix until homogeneous

Assembly Instructions
1. Make baba syrup, set aside to cool
2. Make and bake baba, soak with syrup, set aside.
3. Make coconut pastry cream, pour into desired mold. Freeze until solid.
4. Make pineapple mousse, pour into desired mold.
5. Cut out baba, press into mousse. Freeze until solid.
6. Unmold pineapple mousse, glaze with yellow glaze.
7. Unmold coconut pastry cream, spray with white cocoa butter.
8. Stack coconut pastry cream on pineapple mousse.
9. Garnish with dehydrated pineapple ring.

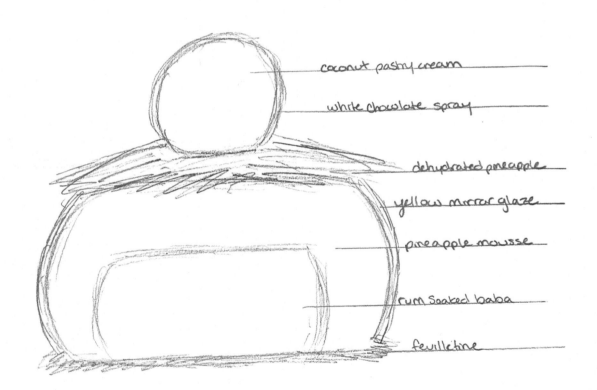

coconut pastry cream

white chocolate spray

dehydrated pineapple

yellow mirror glaze

pineapple mousse

rum soaked baba

feuilletine

Passionfruit

Passionfruit Mousse

Eggs	8 ea
Sugar	600 g
Passion Fruit	340 g
Gelatin	7 ea
Butter	340 g
Whipped cream	320 g

Bloom gelatin in ice water, set aside. Combine eggs, sugar and puree in a pot. Whisk until thickened, remove from heat. Add in bloomed gelatin and butter, set aside until cool. Whip cream to medium peaks, fold into passionfruit base.

Raspberry Compote

Raspberries	2 pints
Water	as needed
Sugar	tt
Lime zest	1 ea
Lime juice	1 ea
Gelatin	3 ea

Bloom gelatin in ice water, set aside. Combine all other ingredients in a pot with enough water to cover the berries. Cook until the raspberries are soft. Add in gelatin. Immersion blend until smooth.

Chocolate Ganache

Chocolate	300 g
Cream	150 g

Place cream in a pot, bring to a boil. Pour over chocolate. Mix until smooth.

Chocolate Sablé

AP Flour	190 g
Cocoa powder	20 g
10X sugar	55 g
Salt	pinch
Butter, cold	150 g
Egg	1 ea
Vanilla	½ tsp

Combine all dry ingredients in a bowl. Add in butter, mix with a paddle attachment until mixture becomes coarse. Add in egg and vanilla. Wrap and chill dough for an hour. Roll out and bake at 350 °F for 15 minutes

Glaze

White chocolate	350 g
Water	150 g
Sugar	300 g
Gelatin	18 g
Condensed milk	300 g
Food color	as needed

Bloom gelatin in ice water. Combine water, sugar, vanilla and condensed milk in a pot, bring to a boil. Add in bloomed gelatin. Pour mixture over white chocolate. Add in yellow food color, mix until homogeneous

Assembly Instructions

1. Make raspberry compote, pour into a pan and freeze until solid.
2. Make chocolate ganache, pour over raspberry compote. Freeze until solid.
3. Make and bake chocolate sablé base.
4. Make passionfruit mousse, pour into desired mold.
5. Punch out ganache and raspberry insert, press into passionfruit mousse. Freeze until solid.
6. Make yellow glaze.
7. Unmold and glaze petit gateaux.
8. Place on chocolate sablé base.
9. Garnish with chocolate feather and raspberry half.

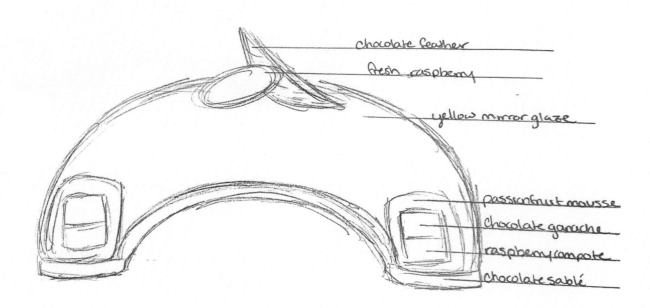

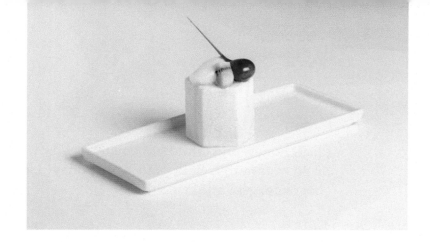

Kiwi Honey

Kiwi Jelly

Sugar	35 g
Water	130 g
Kiwi puree	160 g
Gelatin	8 g

Bloom gelatin in ice water, set aside. Combine water, sugar and puree in a pot. Bring to a boil. Add in bloomed gelatin.

Honey Cheesecake

Cream cheese	8 oz
Lemon zest	1 tsp
Vanilla bean	85 g
Salt	¼ tsp
Cornstarch	1 tbsp
Egg	1 ea

Blend together cream cheese, vanilla, lemon zest and salt in a bowl until smooth. Add in honey, mix until combined. Add in egg and cornstarch, mix until smooth. Bake at 375°F until firm.

Macadamia Nut mousse

Macadamia	¾ C
10X sugar	86 g
Egg whites	15 g
Milk	108 g
Cream	84 g
Sugar	25 g
Vanilla bean	1 ea
Yolks	2 ea
Gelatin	2 ea
Whipped cream	105 g

Combine nuts, 10X sugar and egg whites in a food processor. Grind until a paste is formed, set aside. Bloom gelatin in ice water, set aside. Combine milk, cream, sugar and vanilla in a pot, bring to a boil. Add in egg yolks, cook to 189°F stirring constantly. Add in bloomed gelatin. Pour over macadamia nut paste, emulsify until smooth. Set mixture aside to cool. Whip cream, fold with nut base.

White Chocolate Ganache

White chocolate	113 g
Honey	21 g
Cream	75 g

Place honey and white chocolate in a bowl. Bring cream to a boil, pour over honey and chocolate. Mix until smooth.

Glaze

White chocolate	350 g
Water	150 g
Sugar	300 g
Gelatin	18 g
Condensed milk	300 g
Food color	as needed

Bloom gelatin in ice water, set aside. Combine water, sugar and condensed milk in a pot, bring to a boil. Add in bloomed gelatin. Pour mixture over white chocolate. Add in yellow food coloring. Emulsify until smooth.

Assembly Instructions

1. Make and bake honey cheesecake, freeze until solid.
2. Make kiwi jelly, pour over honey cheesecake, freeze until solid.
3. Make macadamia nut mousse, pour into mold.
4. Punch out kiwi jelly and honey cheesecake insert. Press into macadamia nut mousse, freeze until solid.
5. Make green glaze.
6. Unmold petit gateau, glaze with green glaze.
7. Quenelle ganache and place on top.
8. Garnish with caramelized macadamia nut and fresh kiwi.

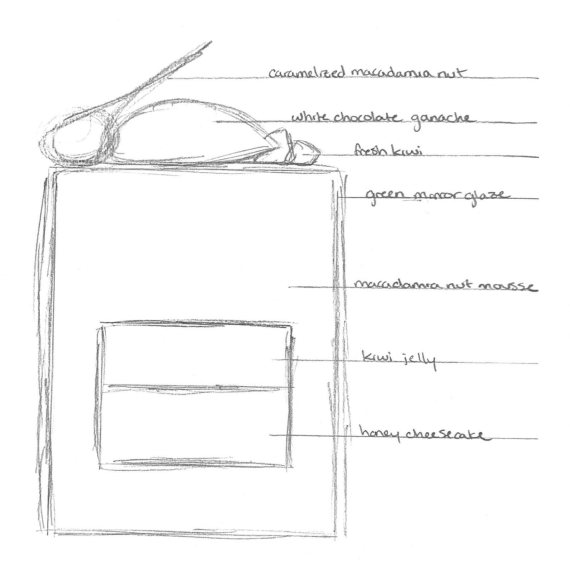

Dragonfruit

Dragon Fruit Cremeux

Dragon fruit	200 g
Sugar (A)	50 g
Cream	250 g
Yolks	80 g
Sugar (B)	60 g
Gelatin	6 g

Bloom gelatin in ice water, set aside. Combine dragon fruit and sugar (A) in a pot, cook until the fruit is soft. Blend until smooth. In a separate pot, boil cream and sugar (B). Temper cream into egg yolks, return to heat. Cook to 189°F stirring constantly. Add in bloomed gelatin. Fold with dragon fruit puree.

Vanilla Lime Bavarois

Cream (A)	183 g
Vanilla bean	2 ea
Egg yolks	40 g
Sugar (A)	17 g
Gelatin	9 g
Egg whites	68 g
Sugar (B)	53 g
Lime zest	1 ea

Bloom gelatin in ice water, set aside. Combine zest, cream, milk and vanilla in a pot. Bring to a boil. In a bowl combine yolks and sugar (A). Temper hot cream into yolk mix, return to heat. Cook until thickened, whisking constantly. Add in bloomed gelatin, set aside to cool. Place egg whites in a bowl, whip until medium peaks form while sprinkling in sugar (B). Fold with cream mixture.

Lime Curd

Butter	84 g
Lime juice	114 g
Sugar	246 g
Eggs	126 g
Gelatin	6 ea

Bloom gelatin in ice water, set aside. Add lime juice and sugar in a pot, bring to a boil. Temper in eggs, return to the heat. Cook until thickened, whisking constantly. Add in bloomed gelatin. Whisk in butter.

Assembly Instructions

1. Make lime curd, pour into the mold. Freeze until solid.
2. Make dragon fruit cremeux, pour over lime curd. Freeze until solid.
3. Make vanilla lime chiboust, pour into desired mold.
4. Punch out curd and cremeux insert, press into chiboust. Freeze until solid.
5. Unmold petit gateaux and spray with pink cocoa butter spray.
6. Garnish with candied dragon fruit slice and gold leaf.

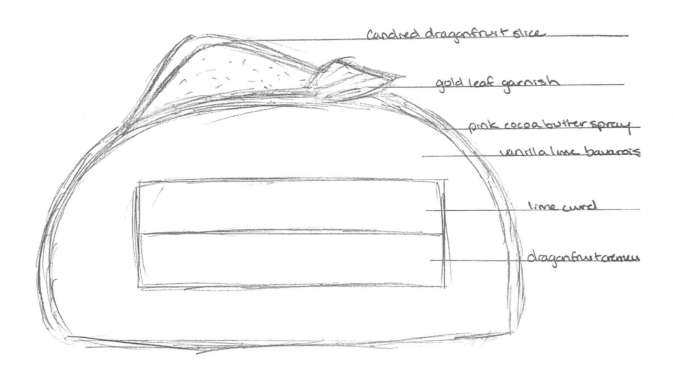

candied dragonfruit slice

gold leaf garnish

pink cocoa butter spray

vanilla lime bavarois

lime curd

dragonfruit cremeux

Coconut Lime

Chocolate Cremeux

Milk	70 g
Cream (A)	45 g
Egg yolks	90 g
Chocolate	160 g
Cream (B)	290 g
Gelatin	3 ea

Bloom gelatin in ice water, set aside. Combine milk and cream (A) in a pot, bring to a boil. Temper into yolks, whisking vigorously. Return to heat, stirring until the mix reaches 189°F. Add in bloomed gelatin. Pour mix over chocolate, blend to emulsify. Whip cream (B) to soft peaks, fold with chocolate mixture.

Coconut Chiboust

Coconut milk	228 g
Sugar (A)	38 g
Salt	pinch
Cornstarch	10 g
Vanilla bean	1 ea
Yolk	1.5 ea
Gelatin	2 ea
Whites	60 g
Sugar (B)	30 g

Bloom gelatin in ice water, set aside. Combine coconut milk, vanilla, salt and half of sugar (A) in a pot, bring to a boil. Combine remaining sugar (A) and yolks. Temper coconut milk mix into yolks, return to heat. Whisk constantly until the mixture thickens. Add in bloomed gelatin. Set aside to cool. Place egg whites in a bowl. Whip while gradually sprinkling in sugar (B) until stiff peaks form. Fold with coconut milk mixture.

Lime Curd

Butter	84 g
Lime juice	114 g
Sugar	246 g
Eggs	126 g
Gelatin	6 ea

Bloom gelatin in ice water, set aside. Add lime juice and sugar in a pot, bring to a boil. Temper in eggs, return to heat. Cook until thickened, whisking constantly. Add in bloomed gelatin. Add in butter.

Chocolate Shell

Chocolate	200 g
Cocoa butter	75 g

Melt chocolate and cocoa butter together in a pot, allow to cool slightly before use.

Assembly Instructions
1. Make chocolate cremeux, pour into a pan. Freeze until solid.
2. Make lime curd, pour over chocolate cremeux. Freeze until solid.
3. Make coconut mousse, pour into desired mold.
4. Cut out lime curd and cremeux center, press into coconut mousse. Freeze until solid.
5. Make chocolate dip.
6. Unmold petit gateaux and dip in the chocolate glaze.
7. Press desiccated coconut around the base.
8. Garnish with dehydrated lime wheel.

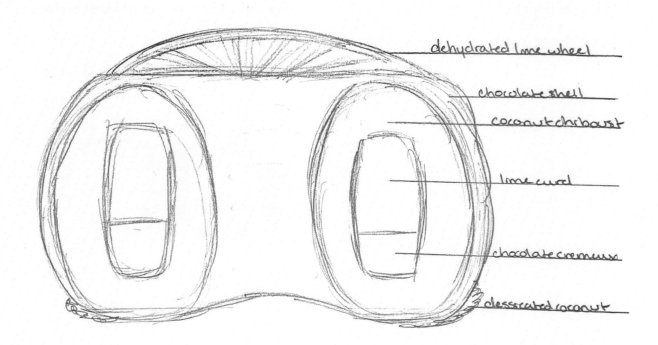

AUTUMN

As the heat from summer begins to cool off we begin leaning towards flavors that bring us warmth and familiarity. This section incorporates seasonal favorites as well as introducing ingredients that one wouldn't immediately associate with fall. Through using classic spices and displaying common desserts in unconventional ways, I hope to redefine the possibilities that the season can bring.

Pumpkin and Coffee

Pumpkin Spice Mousse

Cream	681 g
Brown sugar	102 g
Egg yolks	2 ea
Sugar	75 g
Vanilla	1 tsp
Pumpkin puree	15 oz
Cinnamon	2 tsp
Ginger	½ tsp
Nutmeg	¼ tsp
Cloves	¼ tsp
Whipped cream	300 g
Gelatin	5 ea

Coffee Pastry Cream

Milk	159 g
Cream	97 g
Vanilla	1 tbsp
Instant coffee	50 g
Egg yolks	76 g
Sugar	31 g

Glaze

White chocolate	350 g
Water	150 g
Sugar	300 g
Gelatin	18 g
Condensed milk	300 g
Food color	as needed

Bloom gelatin in ice water, set aside. Heat cream with sugars, spices and vanilla. Bring to a boil. Temper into the egg yolks, return to the heat. Cook to 189°F, add in bloomed gelatin. Pour over pumpkin puree, emulsify to combine. Fold with whipped cream.

Combine coffee powder, milk, cream and vanilla in a pot, bring to a boil. Temper into yolks and sugar. Return to the heat and whisk until thick.

Bloom gelatin in ice water, set aside. Combine water, sugar and condensed milk in a pot, bring to a boil. Add in bloomed gelatin. Pour mixture over white chocolate. Add in yellow food coloring. Emulsify until smooth.

Assembly Instructions
1. Make coffee pastry cream, pour into a pan. Freeze until solid.
2. Make pumpkin spice mousse, pour into desired mold.
3. Punch out coffee pastry cream, press into pumpkin mousse. Freeze until solid.
4. Unmold dessert and glaze with orange glaze.
5. Garnish with chocolate stem.

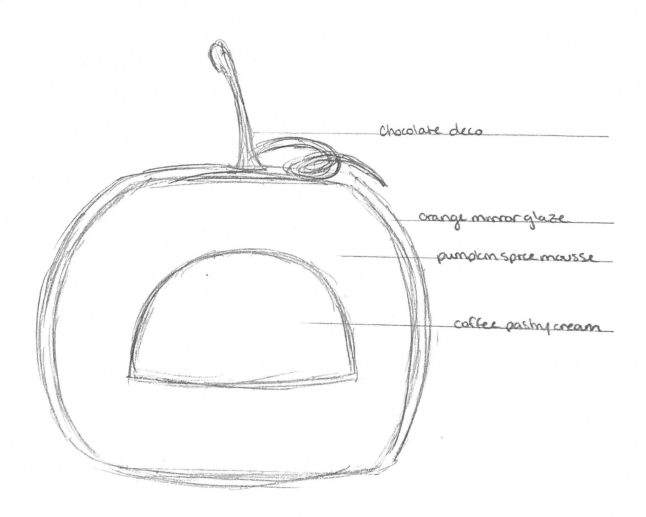

chocolate deco

orange mirror glaze

pumpkin spice mousse

coffee pastry cream

Pistachio Cherry

Orange Mousse

Orange juice	144 g
Orange zest	1 ea
Gelatin	4 ea
Egg whites	70 g
Sugar	144 g
Whipped cream	287 g

Bloom gelatin in ice water, set aside. Heat orange juice and zest in a pot, bring to a boil. Add in boomed gelatin. Place egg whites in a bowl with a whip attachment. In a saucepan heat sugar and enough water to cover until the temp reaches 120°C, stream into whipping egg whites until stiff peaks form. Fold orange mix with meringue and whipped cream.

Pistachio Pastry Cream

Milk	240 g
Vanilla	1 ½ tsp
Egg	1 ea
Sugar	50 g
Cornstarch	2 tbsp
Cubed butter	28 g
Heavy cream	60 g
Pistachios	½ C

Heat milk and vanilla in a saucepan. Bring to a boil. Whisk together egg, cornstarch and sugar in a bowl. Temper the hot milk into the egg mixture, and return to heat. Whisk until the mixture starts to thicken. Whisk in butter and set aside to cool. Fold with whipped cream and ground pistachios.

Cherry Compote

Cherries	8 oz
Lemon zest	1 ea
Lemon juice	1 tbsp
Sugar	24 g
Cornstarch	as needed
Gelatin	2 ea

Bloom gelatin in ice water, set aside. Combine cherries, lemon juice and sugar in a pot, cook on medium heat. Create a slurry with cornstarch and water, add to the cherry mix. Cook until thick. Add in bloomed gelatin.

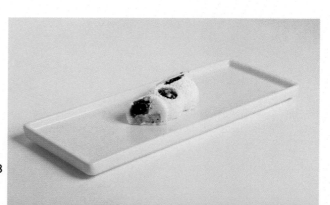

Assembly Instructions

1. Make pistachio pastry cream, pour into a pan. Freeze until solid.
2. Make orange mousse, pour into desired mold.
3. Punch out pistachio pastry cream and press into orange mousse. Freeze until solid.
4. Make cherry compote, set aside to cool.
5. Unmold orange pistachio dessert and spray with white cocoa butter.
6. Garnish with cherry compote and white chocolate decor.

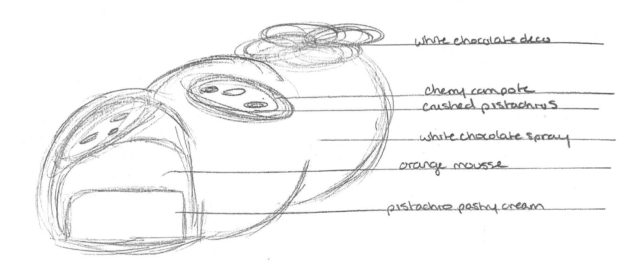

Maple Pecan

Pecan Mousse

Pecans	1 ½ C
10X sugar	173 g
Egg whites	1 ea
Milk	217 g
Cream	168 g
Vanilla bean	1 ea
Sugar	50 g
Egg yolks	4 ea
Gelatin	3 ea
Whipped cream	210 g

Combine pecans, 10X sugar and egg white in a food processor, make a paste. Set aside. Bloom gelatin in ice water. Combine milk, cream and vanilla in a pot, bring to a boil. Temper into egg yolks and sugar. Return to heat and cook to 189°F. Add in bloomed gelatin and emulsify with pecan paste. Fold with whipped cream.

Maple gel

Sugar	35 g
Water	130 g
Maple syrup	160 g
Gelatin	8 g

Bloom gelatin in ice water, set aside. Combine water, sugar and corn syrup in a pot, bring to a boil. Add in bloomed gelatin.

Cinnamon Tuile

Butter	2 tbsp
Brown sugar	2 tbsp
Corn syrup	1 ½ tbsp
AP flour	2 tbsp
Cinnamon	¼ tsp

Melt butter with brown sugar and corn syrup until sugar dissolves. Stir in remaining ingredients off heat. Bake at 375°F.

Glaze

White chocolate	350 g
Water	150 g
Sugar	300 g
Gelatin	18 g
Condensed milk	300 g
Food color	as needed

Bloom gelatin in ice water, set aside. Combine water, sugar and condensed milk in a pot, bring to a boil. Add in bloomed gelatin. Pour mixture over white chocolate. Add in yellow food coloring. Emulsify until smooth.

Assembly Instructions
1. Make maple gel, pour into a pan. Freeze until solid.
2. Make pecan mousse, pour into desired mold.
3. Punch out maple gel and press into pecan mousse. Freeze until solid.
4. Unmold dessert and glaze with tan glaze.
5. Make and bake cinnamon tuile.
6. Garnish with cinnamon tuile and roasted pecan.

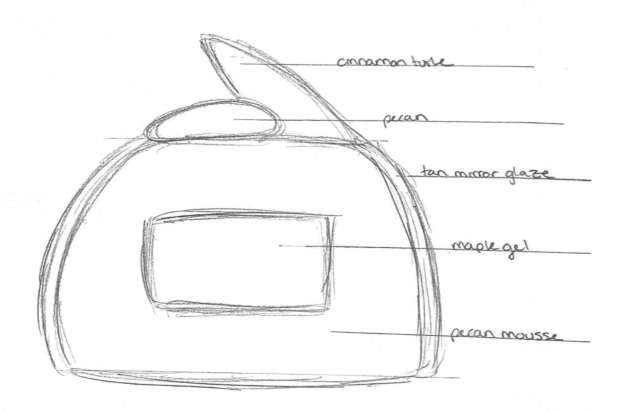

cinnamon tuile

pecan

tan mirror glaze

maple gel

pecan mousse

Cranberry Spice

Vanilla Bean Mousse

Cream (A)	185 g
Vanilla bean	2 ea
Egg yolks	40 g
Sugar (A)	17 g
Gelatin	9 g
Egg whites	68 g
Sugar (B)	53 g

Bloom gelatin in ice water, set aside. Combine cream (A) and vanilla in a pot, bring to a boil. Temper into egg yolks and sugar (A). Return to the heat, cook to 189°F stirring constantly. Add in bloomed gelatin. Whip egg whites with sugar (B) until medium peaks form. Fold the mixtures together.

Cranberry Curd

Cranberries	1 C
Lemon juice	1 tbsp
Egg yolks	3 ea
Sugar	100 g
Butter	57 g
Gelatin	2 ea

Bloom gelatin in ice water, set aside. Combine cranberries and lemon juice in a pot. Cook until the cranberries are soft. Blend to puree, set aside. In a pot combine cranberry puree and sugar, bring to a boil. Temper into egg yolks, return to the heat. Whisk until the mixture thickens. Add in bloomed gelatin and butter

Cinnamon Cheesecake

Cream cheese	8 oz
Sugar	33 g
AP flour	1 tbsp
Eggs	1 ea
Sour cream	80 g
Vanilla	1 tsp
Cinnamon	1 tsp
Nutmeg	½ tsp
Cloves	¼ tsp

Combine cream cheese, flour and sugar until smooth. Add in eggs followed by sour cream, vanilla and spices. Mix until combined. Bake at 300°F for 45min-1 hour or until firm.

Cinnamon Meringue

Egg whites	2 ea	
Maple syrup	152 g	
Salt	pinch	
Cinnamon	1 ¼ tsp	

Place egg whites, syrup and salt in a bowl over a water bath, heat until the mixture is warm. Remove from heat and whip on high until thick and shiny. Gently fold in the cinnamon. Bake at 200°F until dry.

Glaze

White chocolate	350 g	
Water	150 g	
Sugar	300 g	
Gelatin	18 g	
Condensed milk	300 g	
Food color	as needed	

Bloom gelatin in ice water, set aside. Combine water, sugar and condensed milk in a pot, bring to a boil. Add in bloomed gelatin. Pour mixture over white chocolate. Add in yellow food coloring. Emulsify until smooth.

Assembly Instructions
1. Make and bake cinnamon cheesecake, freeze until solid.
2. Make and bake cinnamon spice meringue.
3. Make cranberry curd, pour into desired pan. Freeze until solid.
4. Make vanilla mousse, pour into desired mold.
5. Punch out cranberry curd, press into vanilla mousse. Freeze until solid
6. Unmold cheesecake, glaze with white glaze.
7. Unmold vanilla mousse, glaze with red glaze.
8. Stack the cheesecake on the meringue disc, place on top of the glazed vanilla mousse.

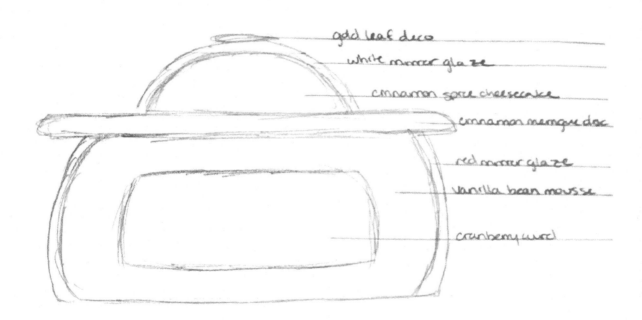

gold leaf deco
white mirror glaze
cinnamon spice cheesecake
cinnamon meringue disc
red mirror glaze
vanilla bean mousse
cranberry curd

Carrot Cake

Spiced Cremeux

Sugar	120 g
Orange zest	1 tbsp
Orange juice	90 g
Cream (A)	120 g
Egg yolks	4 ea
Gelatin	3 ea
Cinnamon	as needed
Nutmeg	as needed
Cloves	as needed
Cream (B)	350 g

Bloom gelatin in ice water, set aside. Combine sugar, orange zest, orange juice, cream (A), cinnamon, nutmeg, and cloves. Bring to a boil. Temper into egg yolks. Add in gelatin. Whip cream (B) to soft peaks, fold with the base.

Carrot Cake

Vegetable oil	107 g
Sugar	75 g
Brown sugar	51 g
Eggs	1 ½ ea
Vanilla	1 tsp
Carrots	1 ¼ C
Baking soda	1 tsp
Salt	¼ tsp
Cinnamon	1 tsp
Nutmeg	¼ tsp
Cloves	pinch
Buttermilk	136 g

Preheat the oven to 350°F. Cream oil and sugars. Add in the eggs and vanilla. Fold in the grated carrots. Combine and add in dry ingredients alternating with the buttermilk. Pour into desired pan, bake for 15-18 minutes.

Carrot Pastry Cream

Egg yolks	4 ea
Milk	380 g
Sugar (A)	100 g
AP flour	2 tbsp
Cornstarch	2 tbsp
Vanilla	1 tbsp
Cinnamon	2 tsp
Nutmeg	½ tsp
Cloves	¼ tsp
Carrots	300 g
Sugar (B)	150 g

Boil carrots with sugar (B) until carrots are soft. Puree, then set aside. Heat milk, vanilla and spices. In a separate bowl combine egg yolks, flour, cornstarch and sugar (A). Temper hot milk into egg mixture, return to heat. Whisk until thick.

Glaze

White chocolate	350 g
Water	150 g
Sugar	300 g
Gelatin	18 g
Condensed milk	300 g
Food color	as needed

Bloom gelatin in ice water, set aside. Combine water, sugar and condensed milk in a pot, bring to a boil. Add in bloomed gelatin. Pour mixture over white chocolate. Add in yellow food coloring. Emulsify until smooth.

Assembly Instructions
1. Make carrot pastry cream, pour into a pan. Freeze until solid.
2. Make and bake carrot cake.
3. Make spiced cremeux, pour into desired mold.
4. Punch out carrot pastry cream and carrot cake, press into spiced cremeux, freeze until solid.
5. Unmold the dessert and glaze.
6. Garnish with cream cheese icing and dehydrated carrot.

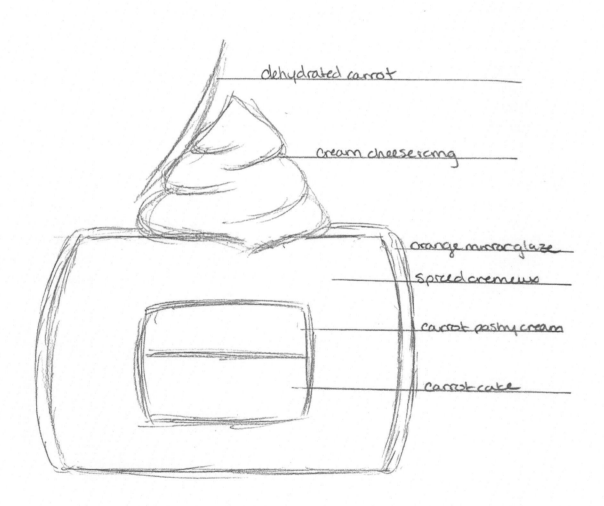

dehydrated carrot

cream cheese icing

orange mirror glaze

spiced cremeux

carrot pastry cream

carrot cake

Caramel Apple

Vanilla Pastry Cream

Vanilla beans	2 ea
Milk	300 g
Egg yolks	2 ea
Sugar	50 g
Cornstarch	2 ½ tbsp
Butter	105 g

Boil milk and vanilla beans in a pot. In a bowl combine yolks, sugar and cornstarch. Temper milk into egg mixture, return to the heat. Whisk constantly until the mixture thickens. Add in cubed butter.

Apple Pie Filling

Apples	3 ea
Lemon juice	½ tbsp
Brown sugar	67 g
Sugar	25 g
Cinnamon	1 tsp
Salt	¼ tsp
Water	180 g
Cornstarch	15 g

Peel and dice apples, toss in lemon juice. Combine brown sugar, sugar, cinnamon, salt, and water in a pot. Stir in apples. Simmer for 10-15 minutes or until the apples are soft. Remove ¼ C of liquid and create a slurry with the cornstarch. Pour into the mixture, cook until thickened.

Graham Sablé

Butter	8 oz
Salt	2 g
Sugar	3.5 oz
Vanilla	1 oz
Graham Cracker	4 oz
Cake flour	7.5 oz
Cinnamon	0.1 oz
Baking Powder	0.1 oz
Egg yolks	1 ½ ea

Cream butter and sugar. Add in egg yolks, vanilla and salt. Add in dry ingredients. Chill the dough for about an hour. Roll out and bake at 350°F.

Caramel Mousse

Gelatin	¼ oz
Sugar	150 g
Glucose	52 g
Cream (A)	190 g
Water	67 ml
Salt	¼ tsp
Cream	375 g
Egg yolks	2 ea

Bloom gelatin in ice water, set aside. In a saucepan, mix together sugar, glucose, salt and water. Cook until it reaches a caramel color. Pour in cream (A). Set aside to cool. Whisk the egg yolks, temper into the caramel. Mix until the temp reaches 82-84°C. Add in bloomed gelatin. Whip remaining cream to soft peaks. Fold cream with caramel.

Glaze

White chocolate	350 g
Water	150 g
Sugar	300 g
Gelatin	18 g
Condensed milk	300 g
Food color	as needed

Bloom gelatin in ice water, set aside. Combine water, sugar and condensed milk in a pot, bring to a boil. Add in bloomed gelatin. Pour mixture over white chocolate. Add in yellow food coloring. Emulsify until smooth.

Assembly Instructions
1. Make and bake graham sablé.
2. Make vanilla pastry cream, pour into mold. Freeze until solid.
3. Make caramel mousse, pour into desired mold.
4. Press vanilla pastry cream into caramel mousse. Freeze until solid.
5. Make apple pie filling, pour into graham sablé shell.
6. Unmold caramel mousse and glaze.
7. Place glazed mousse on top of apple filling.
8. Garnish with gold leaf.

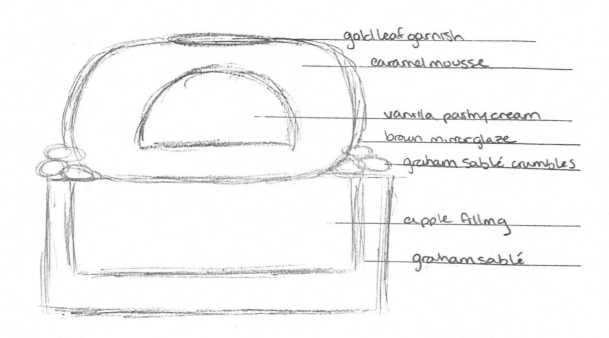

WINTER

As the weather becomes colder, the winter months are able to bring out an assortment of flavor combinations that invoke a feeling of comfort. This section exhibits the use of traditional ingredients for the season but also showcases some elements that wouldn't normally be considered. Combining classic ideas with fun and exciting twists, I hope to bring excitement and intrigue to those cold frosty months.

Gingerbread

Spiced Cremeux

Sugar	120 g
Orange zest	1 tbsp
Orange juice	90 g
Cream	120 g
Egg yolks	4 ea
Gelatin	3 ea
Cinnamon	1 tbsp
Nutmeg	1 ½ tsp
Cloves	½ tsp

Bloom gelatin in ice water, set aside. Combine sugar, orange zest, orange juice, cream and spices in a pot. Bring to a boil, temper into egg yolks. Return to the heat. Cook until the mixture reaches 189°F stirring continuously. Add in bloomed gelatin.

Gingerbread Mousse

Cream (A)	183 g
Vanilla bean	2 ea
Egg yolks	40 g
Sugar	17 g
Gelatin	9 g
Cream (B)	225 g
Molasses	20 g
Ginger	1 ½ tsp
Cinnamon	2 tsp
Cloves	¼ tsp
Nutmeg	1 tsp

Bloom gelatin in ice water, set aside. Combine cream (A), ginger, cinnamon, cloves, nutmeg and vanilla in a pot, bring to a boil. Combine yolks, molasses and sugar. Temper hot cream mix into egg mix, return to the heat. Cook, stirring continuously until mixture reaches 189°F. Add in bloomed gelatin. Whip cream (B) to soft peaks. Fold cream with vanilla mixture.

Gingerbread Dough

Butter	113 g
Brown sugar	150 g
Molasses	113 g
Egg	1 ea
Water	2 tbsp
AP flour	341 g
Baking soda	1 tsp
Salt	½ tsp
Cinnamon	½ tsp
Nutmeg	½ tsp
Allspice	½ tsp

Cream butter and brown sugar until fluffy. Add in molasses, egg and water. Gradually add in dry ingredients. Refrigerate dough for about 30 minutes. Bake at 350°F for about 8-10 minutes.

Assembly Instructions:
1. Make spiced cremeux, pour into a pan. Freeze until solid.
2. Make gingerbread mousse, pipe into desired mold.
3. Punch out spiced cremeux, press into gingerbread mousse. Freeze until solid.
4. Make and bake gingerbread cookies.
5. Unmold petit gateaux, spray with white chocolate cocoa butter spray.
6. Garnish with gingerbread cookie.

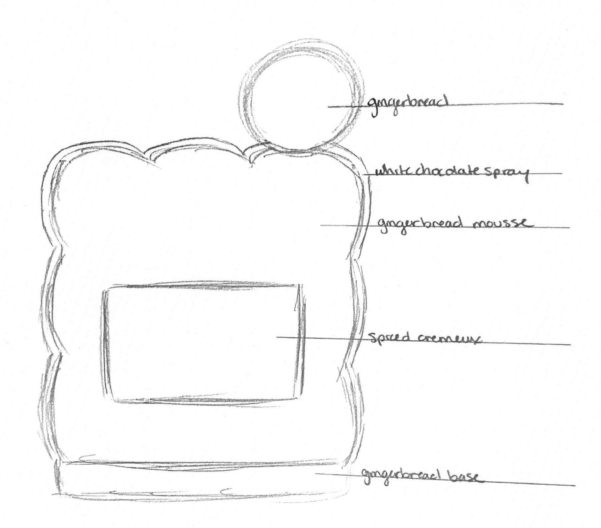

gingerbread

white chocolate spray

gingerbread mousse

spiced cremeux

gingerbread base

Blueberry Pie

Blueberry Cremeux

Blueberries	300 g
Egg yolks	65 g
Egg whites	53 g
Sugar	60 g
Gelatin	3 ea
Softened butter	80 g

Bloom gelatin in ice water, set aside. Cook blueberries in a pot until soft, blend to puree. Bring pureed blueberries and sugar to a boil, temper into the eggs. Return to the heat. Bring to a boil, whisking constantly, remove from heat. Add in gelatin and melted butter.

Blueberry Mousse

Blueberries	95 g
Lemon juice	½ tbsp
Sugar	50 g
Egg yolks	2 ea
Gelatin	16 g
Whipped cream	200 g

Bloom gelatin in ice water, set aside. Cook blueberries until soft, blend to puree. Heat puree, lemon juice and sugar in a pot. Bring to a boil. Temper into egg yolks, return to heat and whisk until thickened. Add in bloomed gelatin, fold with whipped cream.

Vanilla Bavarois

Cream (A)	183 g
Vanilla bean	2 ea
Egg yolks	40 g
Sugar	17 g
Gelatin	9 g
Cream (B)	225 g

Bloom gelatin in ice water, set aside. Combine cream (A) and vanilla in a pot, bring to a boil. Combine yolks and sugar. Temper hot cream mix into egg mix, return to the heat. Cook, stirring continuously until mixture reaches 189°F. Add in bloomed gelatin. Whip cream (B) to soft peaks. Fold cream with vanilla mixture

Chantilly

Cream	150 g	
10X sugar	50 g	
Vanilla bean	1 ea	

Combine all ingredients in a bowl. Whip to stiff peaks.

Glaze

White chocolate	350 g
Water	150 g
Sugar	300 g
Gelatin	18 g
Condensed milk	300 g
Food color	as needed

Bloom gelatin in ice water, set aside. Combine water, sugar and condensed milk in a pot, bring to a boil. Add in bloomed gelatin. Pour mixture over white chocolate. Add in yellow food coloring. Emulsify until smooth.

Graham Sablé

Butter	114 g
Salt	1 g
Sugar	99 g
Vanilla	28 g
Graham cracker	113 g
AP flour	212 g
Cinnamon	3 g
Baking powder	4 g
Egg yolks	30 g

Cream butter and sugar. Add in egg yolks, vanilla and salt. Mix until combined. Sift and add in dry ingredients. Add in graham cracker crumbs. Mix until a dough forms. Wrap and chill dough for 1 hour before use. Roll to ⅛" and cut the desired shape. Bake at 325F for about 8-10 minutes.

Assembly Instructions:
1. Make blueberry cremeux, pour into a tray. Freeze until solid.
2. Make vanilla bavarois, pour over frozen cremeux. Freeze until solid.
3. Make blueberry mousse, Pipe into desired mold.
4. Punch out vanilla and blueberry insert, press into blueberry mousse. Freeze until solid.
5. Make and bake graham sable base.
6. Make purple mirror glaze.
7. Unmold petit gateaux, glaze with purple glaze.
8. Place dessert on graham sable bases.
9. Garnish with chantilly cream and sugared blueberry.

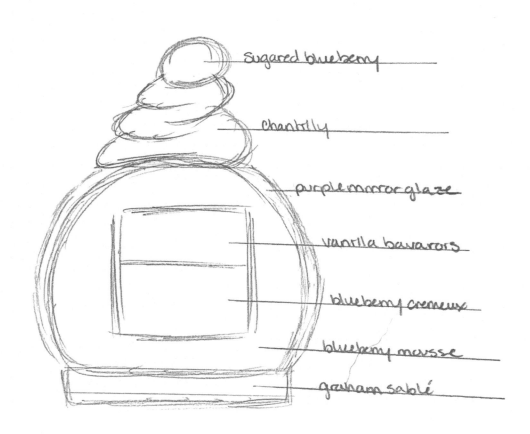

Matcha Blood Orange

Matcha Crumble

Butter, soft	86 g
Sugar	63 g
Ground Almonds	33 g
Matcha powder	1 tbsp
Egg yolk	1 ea
AP flour	156 g
Salt	1 pinch
Whole milk	1 ½ tbsp

Cream butter, sugar, ground almonds and matcha powder. Add in egg yolk. Add in flour and salt. Mix on low while adding in milk until a dough forms. Wrap and chill dough for an hour. Bake at 350°F for 8-10 minutes.

Citrus Cream Cheese

Cream cheese	4 oz
Orange juice	144 g
Orange zest	1 ea
Gelatin	4 ea
Egg whites	70 g
Sugar	144 g
Whipped cream	287 g

Bloom gelatin in ice water, set aside. Place softened cream cheese in a bowl, set aside. Combine orange juice and zest in a pot, bring to a boil. Add in bloomed gelatin. Pour over cream cheese. Mix until homogeneous. In a bowl with a whip attachment, whip egg whites while streaming in sugar until stiff peaks form. Fold with orange mix and whipped cream.

Blood Orange Gel

Sugar	35 g
Water	130 g
Blood orange puree	160 g
Gelatin	8 g

Bloom gelatin in ice water, set aside. Combine sugar, water and blood orange puree in a pot, bring to a boil. Add in bloomed gelatin.

Matcha Cremeux

Gelatin	2 ea
Egg yolks	2 ea
Sugar	100 g
Milk	240 g
Whipped cream	240 g
Matcha powder	1 tbsp
Vanilla	1 tbsp

Bloom gelatin in ice water, set aside. Combine sugar and egg yolks in a bowl. Heat milk, matcha and vanilla in a saucepan, add in bloomed gelatin. Temper the milk into the yolk mixture, and return to heat. Cook to 189°F. Fold with whipped cream.

Glaze

White chocolate	350 g
Water	150 g
Sugar	300 g
Gelatin	18 g
Condensed milk	300 g
Food color	as needed

Bloom gelatin in ice water, set aside. Combine water, sugar and condensed milk in a pot, bring to a boil. Add in bloomed gelatin. Pour mixture over white chocolate. Add in yellow food coloring. Emulsify until smooth.

Assembly Instructions:
1. Make matcha crumble, chill dough.
2. Make matcha cremeux, pour into a pan. Freeze until solid.
3. Make blood orange gel, pour over frozen cremeux.
4. Make citrus cream cheese mousse, pipe into desired mold.
5. Punch out matcha cremeux and blood orange insert, press into cream cheese mousse. Freeze until solid.
6. Make orange glaze.
7. Bake matcha crumble bases.
8. Unmold petit gateaux, glaze with orange glaze.
9. Place desert on matcha crumble base.
10. Garnish with white chocolate deco.

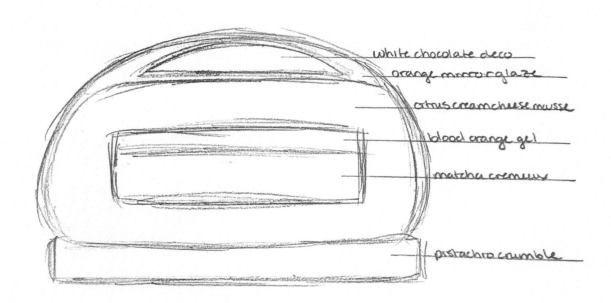

Grapefruit Earl Grey

Milk Chocolate Ganache

Cream	150 g	Boil cream, pour over milk chocolate. Emulsify until smooth.
Milk chocolate	300 g	

Grapefruit Curd

Grapefruit juice	114 g	Bloom gelatin in ice water, set aside. Combine grapefruit juice and sugar in a pot, bring to a boil. Temper into eggs, return to the heat. Whisk continuously until the mixture thickens. Add in bloomed gelatin and butter.
Butter	84 g	
Sugar	246 g	
Eggs	126 g	
Gelatin	6 ea	

Earl Grey Mousse

Milk	183 g	Bloom gelatin in ice water, set aside. Steep the tea in the milk with vanilla bean for 15-20 minutes. Remove tea bags. Bring milk to a boil. Temper into the egg yolks and sugar, return to the heat. Cook mixture to 189°F. Add in bloomed gelatin. Fold with whipped cream.
Earl Grey Tea	3 bags	
Vanilla bean	1 ea	
Egg yolks	40 g	
Sugar	17 g	
Gelatin	9 g	
Whipped cream	300 g	

Citrus Joconde

Egg whites	3 ea
Sugar	135 g
Almond flour	135 g
Eggs	3 ea
AP flour	30 g
Lemon zest	2 ea
Orange zest	1 ea
Butter, melted	23 g

Preheat the oven to 400°F. Whip egg whites on high while streaming in ⅓ of the sugar until stiff peaks form, set aside. Combine almond flour, remaining sugar and whole eggs, whip until thick and smooth. Fold with egg white mixture. Fold in the lemon and orange zests and melted butter. Bake for 10-11 minutes.

Assembly Instructions:
1. Make milk chocolate ganache, reserve in a container.
2. Make and bake citrus joconde, allow it to cool.
3. Make earl grey mousse, pipe into desired mold.
4. Unmold petit gateaux, spray with pink cocoa butter spray.
5. Pour milk chocolate ganache in the center of the mold, freeze.
6. Make grapefruit curd, pour over ganache in the center of the dessert.
7. Place petit gateaux on citrus joconde.
8. Garnish with milk chocolate ganache quenelle and white chocolate deco

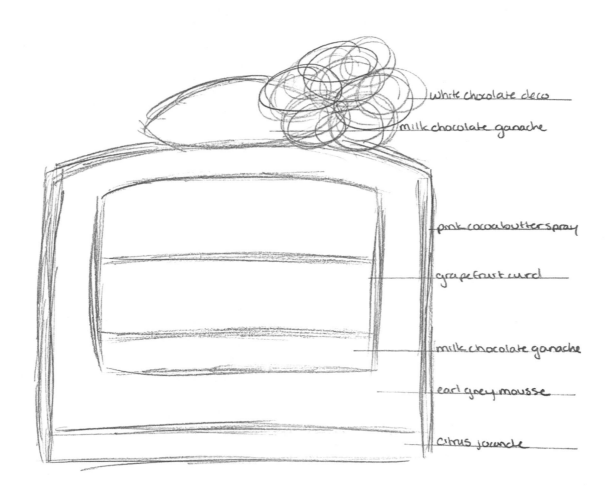

white chocolate deco
milk chocolate ganache

pink cocoa butter spray

grapefruit curd

milk chocolate ganache

earl grey mousse

citrus joconde

Pomegranate

Almond Crumble

AP flour	280 g
Butter	200 g
Almonds	250 g
Sugar	240 g

Cream together room temperature butter and sugar. Sift and add in AP flour. Mix in ground almonds. Wrap and chill the dough. Once chilled, grate the dough and freeze. Bake at 300F.

Pomegranate Mousse

Pomegranate Juice	125 g
Milk	125 g
Egg Yolks	40 g
Sugar	30 g
Gelatin	5 g
Whipped Cream	250 g

Bloom gelatin in ice water, set aside. Boil milk, temper it into the yolks and sugar. Return to heat, cook to 189F. Add in bloomed gelatin. Fold in pomegranate juice. Fold in whipped cream.

Chocolate Cremeux

Milk	70 g
Cream	45 g
Egg Yolks	90 g
Sugar	25 g
Chocolate	160 g
Gelatin	3 ea

Bloom gelatin in ice water, set aside. Bring milk, cream and sugar to a boil. Temper into yolks. Cook, stirring continuously until the mix reaches 189F. Add in bloomed gelatin.

Red Wine Gel

Sugar	35 g
Water	130 g
Red Wine	160 g
Gelatin	8 g

Bloom gelatin in ice water, set aside. Combine water, sugar and wine in a pot, bring to a boil. Add in bloomed gelatin.

Clear Glaze

Sugar	100 g
Water	100 g
Gelatin	3 ea
Gold Luster Dust	

Bloom gelatin in ice water, set aside. Place water and sugar in a pot, bring to a boil for about 5-8 minutes until it appears slightly thicker. Add in bloomed gelatin. Add in gold luster dust, mix until combined

Assembly Instructions:
1. Mix and bake almond crumble, set aside.
2. Make pomegranate mousse, set aside.
3. Make chocolate cremeux, set aside.
4. Make red wine gel, set aside.
5. Alternate layering each component in the mold beginning with the pomegranate mousse followed by the chocolate cremeux and red wine gel.
6. Repeat each layer until the mold is full. Freeze after adding each layer.
7. Unmold, glaze with clear glaze.
8. Place petit gâteaux on almond crumble base.

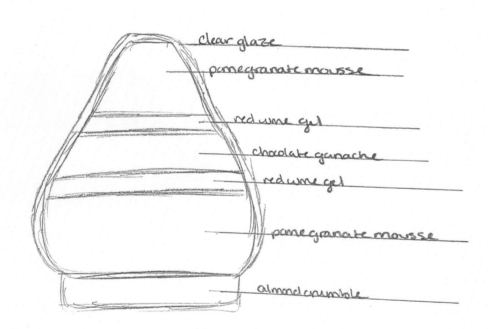

Bananas Foster

Bananas Foster

Brown Sugar	100 g
Butter	57 g
Salt	½ tsp
Cinnamon Stick	1 ea
Bananas	2 ea
Dark Rum	78 g

Combine everything except the bananas and rum in a skillet. Heat until the butter and sugar have melted. Add in the sliced bananas. Simmer for 1-2 minutes. Add in the rum, cook for another minute.

Brown Sugar Mousse

Cream	183 g
Vanilla bean	1 ea
Brown sugar	38 g
Yolks	40 g
Gelatin	9 g
Whipped Cream	240 g
Corn starch	12 g

Bloom gelatin in ice water, set aside. Combine cream, vanilla and brown sugar in a pot. Bring to a boil. In a bowl combine egg yolks and cornstarch. Temper the hot cream mixture into the yolks and starch. Return to the heat. Whisk constantly until the mixture thickens. Add in bloomed gelatin, let cool. Fold with whipped cream.

Chocolate Crumble

AP Flour	188 g
Cocoa Powder	75 g
Salt	¼ tsp
Butter	170 g
Sugar	201 g
Egg	1 ea
Vanilla	1 ½ tsp

Cream the butter and sugar. Add in the egg and vanilla. Sift and add in dry ingredients. Wrap and chill the dough. Bake at 350°F.

Glaze

White chocolate	350 g
Water	150 g
Sugar	300 g
Gelatin	18 g
Condensed milk	300 g
Food color	as needed

Bloom gelatin in ice water, set aside. Combine water, sugar and condensed milk in a pot, bring to a boil. Add in bloomed gelatin. Pour mixture over white chocolate. Add in yellow food coloring. Emulsify until smooth.

Assembly Instructions:
1. Make banana foster filling, pour in desired pan and freeze until solid.
2. Make chocolate crumble, bake bases.
3. Make brown sugar mousse, pour into desired mold.
4. Punch out bananas foster filling, press into brown sugar mousse. Freeze until solid.
5. Make yellow mirror glaze.
6. Unmold petit gateaux, glaze with yellow glaze.
7. Place onto chocolate crumble bases.
8. Garnish with caramelized sugar shard and banana chip.

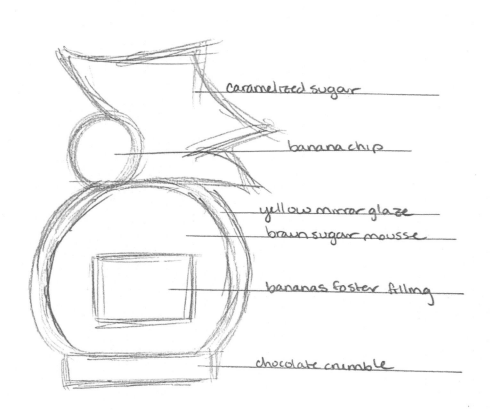

Glossary

Baba: a cake soaked with a spiced rum and sugar syrup.

Bavarois: otherwise known as bavarian cream or crème bavaroise, is a dessert consisting of milk, eggs, vanilla and gelatin combined together with whipped cream.

Bloom Gelatin: placing gelatin sheets in ice water allows the granules to enlarge or "bloom" letting the gelatin dissolve smoothly into the product being made.

Caramelize: the browning of sugar through heat resulting in a sweeter nutty flavor.

Chantilly: whipped heavy cream with the addition of powdered sugar.

Chiboust: a pastry cream or crème pâtissière lightened with whipped cream.

Compote: whole fruit cooked in water with sugar and spices.

Cremeux: French for creamy, it consists of a creme anglaise (or vanilla sauce) combined with dark, white or milk chocolate.

Cross Section: making a straight cut through the center of an object to expose the center.

Curd: a dessert spread or topping usually made with a choice of citrus fruit and thickened with eggs.

Dacquoise: a meringue made with ground nuts folded in and baked.

Diplomat: pastry cream or crème pâtissière folded with whipped cream.

Emulsify: the mixture of two or more substances until evenly dispersed together creating a smooth product.

Ganache: a pastry product made from the combination of heated cream and chocolate.

Gelatin: a water soluble protein used in food to provide support and stabilization of products.

Homogenous: a combination of mixtures that display uniformity of structure and composition. Combining two or more mixtures to create a smooth and uniform new product.

Joconde: a light and airy sponge cake.

Meringue: the product created through stiff beaten egg whites and sugar.

Mousse: typically served chilled, a light dessert with desired flavor and lightened with whipped cream and/or beaten egg white.

Pastry Cream: a thick, creamy custard dessert, also known as crème pâtissière.

Petit Gâteau: individual mousse cake.

Puree: a smooth mixture made with crushed or liquidized fruit.

Rosette: a rose shaped decor.

Sablé: a rich, buttery, stable dough typically used for tart shells.

Slurry: the combination of a starch (usually cornstarch) and cold water used to thicken a sauce.

Temper: slowly bringing up the temperature of a specific ingredient sensitive to heat to prevent it from curdling or cooking too fast.

Tuile: a thin cookie or baked wafer.

Zest: the outer coloured part of a citrus fruit used as flavoring.

Acknowledgments

This book was a lot of hardwork and I could not have completed it without the love and support from everyone. From the bottom of my heart: thank you.

My mom, for all of your endless support and guidance words cannot express how much I appreciate you.

My dad, for your love and advice, I can always rely on you for just about anything.

Amanda, my sister, for your support and kind words throughout this process which were truly appreciated.

Erica, my sister, for your complete confidence in me and my career, I can always count on you.

Isaac, for all your love. I know with complete confidence that I couldn't have written this book without your support. I cannot thank you enough for everything.

Justin, for the truly stunning photos, I am so grateful that you agreed to be a part of this project, thank you.

About the Author

Born and Raised in Mansfield, MA.

Graduated from the Culinary Institute of America in Hyde Park, NY with a bachelors degree in Food Business Management and a concentration in Advanced Pastry.

Participated in Marriott's Voyager program before taking on an Assistant Pastry Sous Chef role at Gaylord Opryland Resort and Convention Center.

Assisted with the grand opening of the Grand Hyatt in downtown Nashville, TN.

Currently the Pastry Sous Chef for M Street Entertainment in Nashville, TN.

Printed in the United States
by Baker & Taylor Publisher Services